Fam

for C 2013 siimas

Barnabas for Children® is a registered word mark and the logo is a registered device mark of The Bible Reading Fellowship

Text copyright © Jane Butcher 2012
Illustrations copyright © Mark Brierley 2012
The author asserts the moral right
to be identified as the author of this work

Published by
The Bible Reading Fellowship
15 The Chambers, Vineyard
Abingdon OX14 3FE
United Kingdom
Tel: +44 (0)1865 319700
Email: enquiries@brf.org.uk
Website: www.brf.org.uk
BRF is a Registered Charity

ISBN 978 0 85746 063 9

First published 2012
10 9 8 7 6 5 4 3 2 1 0
All rights reserved

Acknowledgments
Unless otherwise stated, scripture quotations are taken from the Contemporary English Version of the Bible published by HarperCollins Publishers, copyright © 1991, 1992, 1995 American Bible Society.

A catalogue record for this book is available from the British Library

Printed in Singapore by Craft Print International Ltd

The paper used in the production of this publication was supplied by mills that source their raw materials from sustainably managed forests. Soy-based inks were used in its printing and the laminate film is biodegradable.

Family Fun for Christmas

30 Advent and Christmas activities for families to share

Jane Butcher

To Chris and Jess Rees for the years
of friendship and godparenting
enjoyment

With grateful thanks to the
Mayandithevars, Konecnys, Cornishes,
Witheridges and Dixies for their
international contributions
and ideas

Contents

Foreword

Once again Jane Butcher excels with *Family Fun for Christmas*, giving families ideas to ensure that the Christian significance of this key Christian festival becomes part of family ritual during the festive season.

These rituals are like the stitching holding together the fabric of faith as children grow up. They are the rituals our children will want to repeat in their own families as, we trust, they pass on real and living faith to the next generation.

These simple games and activities are ideal for families with or without a strong Christian heritage. And where Messy Church is introducing families to faith from completely unchurched backgrounds, Jane's creative ideas will help the whole family to grasp the wonder of Christmas from a Christian perspective.

Catherine Butcher

Introduction

Advent and Christmas—what words spring to mind? Excitement, fun, holiday, shopping... or simply panic? Without a doubt it can be a busy time of preparation, whether that be in shopping, cooking or attending school or work events, but it is also a time to prepare for the real celebration—the birth of Jesus.

For Christians, Advent is the time of preparation for Christmas in the same way that Lent is the preparation for Easter. Within Advent we find the accounts of the Angel Gabriel appearing to Zechariah to announce the gift of their son John, and to Mary to announce the gift of Jesus, the journey to Bethlehem, the search for a birthplace and other events leading up to the birth of Jesus.

Going beyond Christmas itself, we move into Epiphany, celebrated in January, which marks the arrival of the wise men or Magi bringing gifts to Jesus.

Throughout this book there are ways to learn more, have fun and celebrate this Christian season together as a family in your home. Whether you prefer cookery, craft, construction, challenges or chatting, there are activities involving all of these for all ages.

The ideas can be used as best suits your family. You may choose to do something each week at a set family time together or dip into the book at various times during the week—the choice is yours. However you choose to use it, we hope you will enjoy celebrating together all that the season offers.

Jane Butcher

Activities

1. Pack it in!

This activity is about finding the meaning of Christmas with so much going on.

It can be done individually or in groups, depending how many boxes you have.

Give each member of the family or group an empty cereal box, either family or variety pack size. Alternatively you could use a large sweet box.

Place in the bottom a very small gift, wrapped simply in a small piece of paper or kitchen roll. Ideas could include a sweet, satsuma, rubber—the same in each box and enough for each person in the group.

Take some pages of newspaper or magazine. Each person/group has to fit as many pages into the box as possible. Is it better to fold neatly or cram madly? At the end, take them out, counting how many each person/group managed to squeeze in. Then take out the 'hidden treasure' and unwrap.

Discuss together how we can sometimes cram a lot into Christmas, but the heart of Christmas is that God gave a tiny hidden treasure wrapped in cloths—the baby Jesus.

What can you do this Christmas to remember this?

Can you use the ideas in this book to help?

2. Make an Advent calendar

Buy 24 round gift tags, one for each day from 1 December to Christmas Eve. On the back of each one, write a word or words from the Christmas story. Ideas could include: Angel Gabriel, John, Mary, Joseph, carpenter, Herod, census, soldiers, Nazareth, Bethlehem, innkeeper, Jesus, manger, hay, animals, shepherds, wise men, star, gifts, gold, frankincense and myrrh.

Optional: Attach a small wrapped chocolate to the front of each decoration using Blu-Tack or low-adhesive sellotape or Micropore™ tape to avoid damage when removed.

Hang them on your tree or place them in the centre of the dining table; or, if you feel more creative, you could create your own Advent mobile by hanging them from coat hangers. Mix them up to avoid clustering similar words together such as gold, frankincense and myrrh. Select one decoration each day from the beginning of Advent. Choose who will have the chocolate (if using), and read the word or words on the back. Discuss as a family where it appears in the story. If you don't know, take time to look it up in a Christmas storybook or children's Bible. The Christmas story can be found at the beginning of the book of Luke.

3. Christmas decorations

Names of Jesus

Buy some round gift tags. On the back of each one, write one of the names given to Jesus. For example, you could choose 'Saviour', 'Light of the World' or 'Messiah'. The book of Isaiah gives some ideas:

> A child has been born for us. We have been given a son who will be our ruler. His names will be Wonderful Adviser and Mighty God, Eternal Father and Prince of Peace. His power will never end; peace will last for ever. He will rule David's kingdom and make it grow strong. He will always rule with honesty and justice. The Lord All-Powerful will make certain that all of this is done.
>
> Isaiah 9:6–7

You could either attach them individually to your Christmas tree or string them together to make a decoration banner.

Hanging star

Take some long, coloured chenille sticks or pipe cleaners. Make two triangles and interlock them by feeding the point of one through the other. Hang as a decoration using thick string or cord attached to the top point of the triangle.

Where in the Christmas story does it mention a star or stars?

Candleholders

A candle is often part of Christian worship. At Christmas time, Christians remember that Jesus came to be the 'light of the world'. As a family you could decorate your table with your own candleholder and candle.

Take a small plastic flowerpot or yoghurt container and decorate it with gold spray paint. Place a small piece of florist's foam in the centre and cover with foil (to catch the wax). Push a small candle in a candle holder into the centre through the foil into the foam. Decorate the base of the candle and/or the pot with leaves, holly or berries, but take care that your decoration is not too near the flame. Light the candle at mealtimes to remember that Jesus came to be the Light of the World.

4. A family Christingle

The Christingle was established by the Moravian Church in 1747 as a symbol of Christ's light and love. Details of how to make one can be found at http://www.childrenssociety.org.uk/what-you-can-do/fundraising-and-appeals/christingle/what-christingle

or you can follow the instructions over the page.

1. Take an orange and slice a small amount from the bottom so that it will stand on a plate or flat surface. The orange represents the world.
2. Fasten a piece of red tape or ribbon around the middle using some sticky tape. The red ribbon represents the love or the blood of Christ.
3. Lay a small square of silver foil on top.
4. Use a birthday candle and holder and push the holder firmly through the foil into the orange to hold the candle securely (the wax will drip on to the foil). The candle reminds us that Jesus is the light of the world.
5. Load four cocktail sticks with raisins, sultanas, cherries or soft sweets, and make sure that the points are covered. Insert them around the base of the candle. These represent the four seasons and the fruits of the earth—God's good gifts to us.
6. Place the Christingles on a plate or flat surface. When you sit down to eat together, light the candle. Think of one thing that you would like to thank God for, for example your home, friends, family, teachers or work colleagues.

5. Special as snowflakes!

Christmas is often associated with cold weather and snow. It is said that no two snowflakes are the same. In the same way no two people are the same: we have different personalities, different things we are good at, and everyone, even identical twins, has a different fingerprint.

Make a family fingerprint frame. Each person can press their thumb and/or fingers in some paint or onto an ink pad and place it on a piece of card, and then share with the rest of the family one thing that they feel makes them special or unique.

You could place the frame somewhere in your home to remind you of how special you all are.

6. Sign language names

An angel from the Lord appeared to Zechariah at the right side of the altar. Zechariah was confused and afraid when he saw the angel. But the angel told him:

'Don't be afraid, Zechariah! God has heard your prayers. Your wife Elizabeth will have a son, and you must name him John. His birth will make you very happy, and many people will be glad.'

Luke 1:11–14

When the Angel Gabriel appeared to Zechariah to tell him he was going to have a son, Zechariah found it hard to believe, and because of this he wasn't able to speak for several months. How do you think he might have communicated with his friends and family? Do you think he could have used sign language?

The first words he said when he could speak again were to tell everyone that his son's name was going to be John. Can you find out how to say your name in sign language? You could find out by looking in a book from the library or on the internet, or by asking someone who knows sign language.

7. Christmas story word search

```
            I
          L N E
          B N L
        F Q K T K
        A H E M C
      G V Z E I I X
      U A P P R X K
    M A R Y E V O P A
    H G R I R T M D T
  K Y I G R S I H O N M
  T E L I Z A B E T H J
  E F L O M N A P F O B
H W I S E M E N H S X P S
H U D A M G S Z E V C U Y
C U S Y W T N P P E I H N
T G J I Z E C H A R I A H P B
          B
      P M V B C
      E D G B E
      J E S U S
      F Q G X C
```

ANGEL	JOSEPH
ELIZABETH	MARY
HEROD	WISE MEN
INNKEEPERS	ZECHARIAH
JESUS	

(Solution on page 56.)

8. Flap the donkey race

Mary travelled from Nazareth to Bethlehem, and tradition tells us that she may have travelled on a donkey. You will need two pictures of a donkey, either drawn or printed out on lightweight card or paper. Take four pieces of paper. Write Nazareth on two pieces and Bethlehem on the other two. Place them equal distances apart and place the donkey just in front of the Nazareth sign.

You will also need a folded newspaper as your 'flapper'.

Either in teams or one against one, wave your newspaper up and down to flap the donkey along in the journey from Nazareth to Bethlehem. Who will get the donkey there first? If you are working in teams: once the donkey has arrived in Bethlehem, pick up the donkey and bring it back to Nazareth for the next person. Repeat until everyone has had a turn. If you have uneven numbers, one person will need to go twice in the team with fewer people.

9. Centurion soldier's armour

The centurion soldiers would have been collecting information for the census when Joseph and Mary arrived in Bethlehem. Make breastplates out of a cardboard box and swords from the inside of a roll of kitchen foil or cling film.

The soldiers were taking information, not fighting, so when you have your armour on, ask family members questions about their full names, the names of their parents, brothers, sisters and so on. If appropriate to your family, you may even want to write it down and make a family tree together.

10. Build the Nativity

Throughout Advent you could build the Christmas story. Start at the part of the story where Mary and Joseph travel to Bethlehem. You will find this in the book of Luke, chapter 2.

About that time Emperor Augustus gave orders for the names of all the people to be listed in record books. These first records were made when Quirinius was governor of Syria.

Everyone had to go to their own home town to be listed. So Joseph had to leave Nazareth in Galilee and go to Bethlehem in Judea. Long ago Bethlehem had been King David's home town, and Joseph went there because he was from David's family.

Mary was engaged to Joseph and travelled with him to Bethlehem. She was soon going to have a baby, and while they were there, she gave birth to her firstborn son. She dressed him in baby clothes and laid him on a bed of hay, because there was no room for them in the inn.

Luke 2:1–7

Select an area in the house to become the 'stage' where the scene will build throughout Advent. Each week, read the next part of the story and add items that relate to that part of the story until by Christmas you have completed the scene. You could use Lego®, Playmobil®, dolls or knitted figures for the characters.

Junk modelled stable

Use items from around your house to build a small stable. These could include a cut-down cereal box or teabag box to make the base and/or sides, and the top of an egg carton as a roof. Once it is built, read the part of the Christmas story where Mary and Joseph arrive at the stable and Mary gives birth to Jesus.

What words would you use to describe how the stable might look... smell... feel?

Soft toy stable

For younger children, recreate the stable scene with soft toy animals or a favourite doll wrapped in a blanket or pillowcase and placed in a box. The child could dress up as Mary, Joseph or a shepherd—a tea towel as a headdress is fine!

Make your own crib

We read in the Christmas story that the wise men brought gifts to the baby Jesus when he was in his crib. Fill a small box or cake baking case with some shredded paper, hay or straw if available, or even crushed-up Shredded Wheat®. Place a small chocolate figure or jelly baby in the 'crib'.

11. Christmas carols

Carol quiz

As a family, how many carols can you think of that mention:

- the name of Jesus?
- the word 'manger'?
- the word 'star(s)'?

Write your own

Choose one of your favourite Christmas carols. Using the same tune, write another verse together. It could be about Christmas or about members of your family or things that have happened in the past year.

Quick fire fun!

As a family, answer the following questions in turn, saying the first answer that comes into your head. Try not to spend too long thinking about it.

Which is your favourite carol?
Which carol do you think is the liveliest?
Which carol do you think is hardest to sing?

Christmas carol word search

```
Q Y M X G Y W W J W M U G J R X L P Q J W H Q
R M X H R U N X D K C W U Q S C X K K C N N Z
Z X D T Y B I R L E H W E V M P B A D B K P F
O F G H A I V H W C C F P T H K V Z P V E E M
T H G I N T N E L I S K T N H N S T C Q S Y R
B K L X J N N N J R K N T K P R G W A X D V Z
D R A G H B A S G P W D E H P N E Z C N D S T
A V I S O C F I E X Z T W V E I N E B B M G P
C P D S M G R O K S C A Z D J H J Q K D S R I
N W O T E L T T I L O O H A O L A P E I F V C
G B B G U N I O L L W Q T W L C V L G X N P J
G K W N B F U G Q L A C B P A S X X L K Q G J
A W A Y I N A M A N G E R N M A E N I S G I S
D I N G D O N G M E R R I L Y O N H I G H E X
G N I S S L E G N A D L A R E H E H T K R A H
O N C E I N R O Y A L D A V I D S C I T Y T L
K B L L K N N G S B T E W M G I S C F Q E V Z
T J H C B B I J A V S L Y R E P C Y C A D B I
A Y W X Z W H V E G Y Z A H G B M R C B V A V
H M A Z V U L V U P H S N I X K X P H S I R P
X W K K O C O M E A L L Y E F A I T H F U L X
O Q J N N T H E F I R S T N O W E L L O Y Q V
C F I R K L V U G T Z J P M D Z Z G S B F T I
```

AWAY IN A MANGER
DECK THE HALLS
DING DONG MERRILY ON HIGH
HARK THE HERALD ANGELS SING
O COME ALL YE FAITHFUL
O LITTLE TOWN
ONCE IN ROYAL DAVID'S CITY
SILENT NIGHT
THE FIRST NOWELL
WE THREE KINGS

(Solution on page 57.)

12. Treasure hunt

Hide items related to the Christmas story (star, wrapped gift, toy animals, home-made crib) around the house for children to find. You could offer a prize at the end. Fun for all ages but particularly suitable for younger children.

13. Word hunt

Using gift tags, write one word on each tag and hide them around the house. Children have to find them and put the words in the right order to complete the sentence.

For younger children you could use:

> Christmas is when Jesus was born
> Jesus was born to be our friend

For older children:

> Jesus was born to be our saviour
> Bethlehem was the place of Jesus' birth

Or, to make it a little more difficult:

> This day in David's town a Saviour has been born (Luke 2:11)

14. Wordmaker

As individuals, teams or the whole family, see how many words you can make from the word 'Christmas' or 'Bethlehem', using each letter only once.

For a longer challenge, try 'Journey to Bethlehem'.

Christmas traditions from around the world

We have Christmas traditions in the UK such as Christmas trees, Christmas pudding, mince pies and Brussels sprouts. Many families have their own individual traditions.

Families in other countries also have traditions that may be very different from ours. Why not 'visit' some other traditions during Advent? You could 'travel' to another country by trying new recipes, crafts and activities together. Here are some ideas.

Christmas in New Zealand

Christmas falls in the middle of summer in New Zealand. Some traditions are similar to those in the UK, while others are quite different.

For example, as well as the Christmas fir tree, a red Christmas tree called the Pohutukawa tree is also popular. Why not look it up on the internet to see what it looks like?

15. Summertime Christmas dinner

As the weather is so hot, Christmas dinner would be a barbecue or a ham salad followed by fruit salad and ice cream. How does that sound to you?

Why not try this meal during Advent? How does it feel to be eating these during our winter?

16. Design a 'summer' Christmas card

In New Zealand they send Christmas cards, but these would show a summer scene, not a winter one. As a family, could you design a summer Christmas card? What would you include?

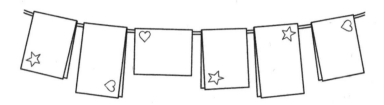

Christmas in Southern India

Many houses are decorated with colourful decorations. Inside the house there are colourful paper loops linked together to form a paper chain. People may also twist coloured crepe paper to make a twisted chain decoration. The outside of the house would be decorated with lights. Christians would have a star outside their house, and some would also have a clay pot with a candle inside. Both the star and the candle are symbols that Jesus is the light of the world.

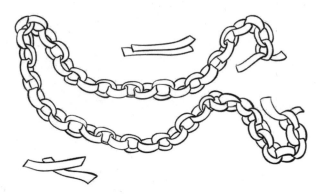

17. Paper decorations

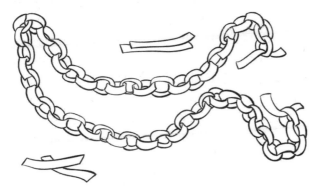

Paper chains

Buy some gummed paper links from a craft or toy shop. As a family, lick, link and stick the loops together to form a chain and use this to decorate the room.

Paper twists

Buy some crepe paper strands from a craft or toy shop. Ask one person to hold one end whilst another gently twists the strand. Secure to a wall or door frame with Blu-Tack®, or a drawing pin if you don't mind leaving a pin hole.

18. Glitter stars

Cut out a star shape in thick card. Poke a thin hole through the top point of the star. Add glue to one side of the card and sprinkle with gold glitter. Allow to dry. Repeat on the other side if you want both sides covered. Thread a piece of string or cord through the hole and hang your star in a window.

19. Clay candle pots

Buy some self-hardening clay (available from craft and toy shops) and mould into a pot shape. When it is hard paint the outside in the colour(s) of your choice and place a tea light inside. Always ask an adult to light the tea light and don't forget to blow it out!

Southern Indian worship and food

Christians in Southern India go to church on Christmas Eve and then again on Christmas Day from 4.00 to 6.30am!

Later in the day they eat something like a chicken or lamb biryani.

As a sweet dish, they often eat a rice dish called Semiya Payasam. Why not have a go at making this together?

20. Southern Indian Christmas rice

1 cup of vermicelli
¾ cup of water
1 cup of sugar
A pinch of turmeric
1 cup of milk
7–8 raisins
½ tsp cardamom powder

1. Fry the vermicelli in butter or oil until brown.
2. Boil the water and add to the vermicelli.
3. Cook until soft. (Don't drain the water.)
4. Add the milk, sugar, raisins, cardamom and turmeric.
5. Simmer for two minutes.
6. Serve hot.

Christmas in the Czech Republic

The main celebration takes place on Christmas Eve. Children help to decorate the Christmas tree with candles, baubles, wooden toys, glitter, red apples, gingerbread cookies and chocolate figures.

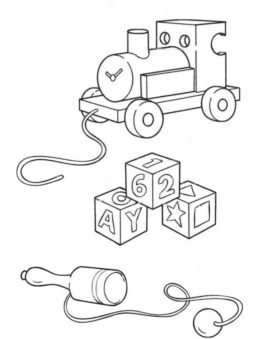

After the evening meal the family gathers in the living room, where real candles have been lit on the tree. Underneath or near the tree is a large pile of nicely wrapped presents. The family sing a selection of traditional Christmas carols and then the youngest child is allowed to give the presents out. The children believe that the presents come from baby Jesus to make them happy and as his generous response to having received presents from the shepherds and kings when he was born. At this point people also help themselves to delicious homemade Christmas cookies (*vanocni cukrovi* in Czech). Each family tends to pass their family recipes from generation to generation, typically making around seven varieties before Christmas.

Make some cookies and sit together to sing some carols or do the Christmas Carol quiz from this book before eating them. Here are two recipes to use.

21. Linz cookies

500g flour
250g sugar
2 egg yolks
320g butter

1. Mix all the ingredients into a biscuit dough and let it rest in the fridge overnight.
2. Roll the dough until it is a few millimetres thick. Using one half of the dough, cut out round or star shapes. From the other half cut out the same shapes, but with a small round or star-shaped hole cut from the centre of the cookie for decoration.
3. Lay the shapes on a greased baking tray and bake in a pre-heated oven at Gas Mark 3/170°C/325°F for approximately 7–10 minutes. The cookies are ready when they turn slightly brown.
4. When the shapes cool down, take one cookie without a hole, spread it with a fine layer of strawberry jam (or another flavour of your choice) and place a cookie with a hole in the top so that you can see the jam through the hole.

22. Vanilla crescents

240g flour
A pinch of salt
160g butter
1 egg yolk
100g ground walnuts (optional—beware nut allergies)
50g icing sugar
Vanilla sugar for coating

1. Mix the flour, salt, butter, egg yolk and walnuts into a dough and let it rest in the fridge overnight.
2. Roll the dough into 4–5cm strips and bend them to form crescents.
3. Bake at Gas Mark 3/170°C/325°F for approximately 10 minutes until golden brown.
4. While warm, coat generously in a mix of icing sugar and vanilla sugar.

Christmas in Chile and Argentina

In some ways Christmas celebrations in Argentina and Chile are similar to those in the UK in that people decorate a tree, have family meals and give gifts. They wish each other Merry Christmas, which in Spanish is 'Feliz Navidad!'

However, there are several differences.

Christmas trees are decorated using lace and balls. The nativity scene is often arranged beneath the tree.

The weather is very hot, as it is summertime there.

The main celebration takes place on Christmas Eve. There is often a big party at home or people visit family and/or friends enjoying barbecues, green salads and potato salads wherever they go. Desserts include panettone, which is a sweet bread, or turrons, which are sweets, and fruit salad.

An extremely popular preserve that is used as a filling in many pastries, cakes and sweets is dulce de leche.

Why not make some as a family?

23. Dulce de leche

1 litre milk
300g sugar
Vanilla pod or vanilla essence (to taste)

1. Boil milk and sugar with vanilla pod or essence, together with a pinch (less than a quarter of a teaspoon) of bicarbonate of soda, over a high heat until the milk has a little colour.
2. Continue cooking over a low heat, barely simmering, until it thickens.
3. Stir frequently to avoid it sticking to the bottom. This will take about two hours.

Or the easy way!

Slowly boil a tin of sweetened condensed milk, unopened, for two hours. Make sure you keep plenty of boiling water in the pan. Allow to cool. It will be honey-coloured and can be spread on bread or cakes.

If cooked for three hours, it can be served sliced—it's delicious with banana.

After the meal there may be fireworks, and presents are often exchanged and opened.

Christmas Day is often very quiet, with people attending church and visiting family and friends.

Another big celebration takes place on 6 January, when Epiphany is celebrated. This is when Christians remember that the wise men followed a star to find the baby Jesus. Children will often leave out water, carrots and hay for the camels and a pair of their shoes. In the morning they may find gifts or sweets in the shoes as a gift from the three wise men.

24. Edible hay bales

Why not make some edible hay bales for the camels?

250g shredded wheat or similar cereal
200g chocolate

1. Slowly melt the chocolate in the microwave or in a bowl over a pan of simmering water. Don't let the bowl touch the water.
2. Crush up the cereal and mix into the melted chocolate.
3. Shape into small square bales of hay.
4. Leave to cool for two hours or place in the fridge.

25. New Year!

Epiphany is celebrated in many countries including the UK on 6 January. It is when Christians remember the wise men who visited the baby Jesus. They saw a star rising in the East and realised that it was a sign that the King of the Jews had been born. They followed the star to Bethlehem, where they found the baby Jesus and gave him gifts of gold, frankincense and myrrh.

Read the story of the wise men visiting Jesus (see over the page).

26. Sleeping under the stars

The wise men had to travel a long way. Have you ever thought about where they slept on the journey? In those days there wouldn't have been as many hotels or B&Bs around. Could they have slept in the fields under the stars, or under a tent or shelter they made themselves?

Set up your own shelter in your bedroom or living room. You could use chairs or other furniture to support some blankets or sheets as a cover. It may not be wise to sleep in there, but why not sit inside and read the part of the story (below) when the wise men visit Jesus.

When Jesus was born in the village of Bethlehem in Judea, Herod was king. During this time some wise men from the east came to Jerusalem and said, 'Where is the child born to be king of the Jews? We saw his star in the east and have come to worship him.'

When King Herod heard about this, he was worried, and so was everyone else in Jerusalem. Herod brought together the chief priests and the teachers of the Law of Moses and asked them, 'Where will the Messiah be born?'

They told him, 'He will be born in Bethlehem, just as the prophet wrote,

"Bethlehem in the land of Judea, you are very important among the towns of Judea. From your town will come a leader, who will be like a shepherd for my people Israel." '

Herod secretly called in the wise men and asked them when they had first seen the star. He told them, 'Go to Bethlehem and search carefully for the child. As soon as you find him, let me know. I want to go and worship him too.'

The wise men listened to what the king said and then left. And the star they had seen in the east went on ahead of them until it stopped over the place where the child was. They were thrilled and excited to see the star.

When the men went into the house and saw the child with Mary, his mother, they knelt down and worshipped him. They took out their gifts of gold, frankincense, and myrrh and gave them to him. Later they were warned in a dream not to return to Herod, and they went back home by another road.

Matthew 2:1–12

27. What's my name?

The names of the three wise men were Caspar, Melchior and Balthasar. Casper means Master-of-Treasure, Melchior means King and Balthasar means Protect-the-King.

Do you know what your name means? Take time either to look in a book or go online to find out what your name means. Do the same for each member of your family.

What are your favourite boys' and girls' names? What do they mean?

28. New Year star party

Make star-shaped sandwiches and cookies using star-shaped cookie cutters. Have you ever tried star fruit? See if you can find some to include on this party menu.

Basic shortbread biscuit recipe

225g plain flour
175g butter
75g caster sugar

1. Cream together the butter and sugar.
2. Sift in the flour and mix together with a spoon.
3. Mould the mixture into a ball with your hands. If it isn't holding together, add a little milk to help it bind.
4. Place on a floured board or surface and roll out to a thickness of about 3mm.
5. Cut into star shapes using cookie cutters.
6. Place on a greased baking tray and bake at Gas Mark 2/150°C/300°F for 15–20 minutes until golden brown.

An alternative idea is to bake or buy some small round biscuits and decorate them with icing and small chocolate stars from the home baking section of the supermarket.

29. Give a gift

The wise men brought gifts to Jesus. Can you remember what gifts they brought... and can anyone spell them?

Wrap a small box in gold-coloured wrapping paper, and place it in the centre of your family or group of friends. If you were a wise man, what precious gift would you bring to the baby Jesus? Let each person answer in turn.

If someone were to give you a precious gift, what would it be—a gift of happiness, peace, friendship or something else?

30. Guidelines for life

If you could suggest to Baby Jesus three things that would help him through life, what three things would they be? Examples might include 'being kind to others' or 'spending time with your closest friends'.

What are your three most important resolutions for the year ahead?

Also from Faith in Homes

Family Fun for Easter

30 Lent and Easter activities for families to share

Jane Butcher

Family Fun for Easter will help you to share the meaning of Lent and Easter with your children in 30 'family moments', to explore faith in the home, and to have lots of fun together in the process! The activities are structured to take the family through the season of Lent from Shrove Tuesday to Easter Day, including Mothering Sunday.

'A lovely, easy guide to Easter celebration.'

Michele Guinness, author and speaker

ISBN 978 0 85746 049 3   £4.99

You can view all our current titles at our BRF Online Shop: www.brfonline.org.uk.

Family Fun for Summer

30 holiday activities for families to share

Jane Butcher

Summer time, the longer days and school holidays offer more time for families to spend time together to talk, play and reconnect with one another in the midst of busy family life. *Family Fun for Summer* provides thirty 'fun on a budget' activities to help you to spend quality time with your children over the summer, to explore faith in the home, and to have lots of fun together in the process!

'Just what every family needs.'

Michele Guinness, author and speaker

ISBN 978 0 85746 061 5   £4.99

You can view all our current titles at our BRF Online Shop. www.brfonline.org.uk.

Christmas story word search solution

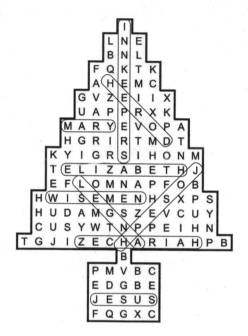

ANGEL   JOSEPH
ELIZABETH   MARY
HEROD   WISE MEN
INNKEEPERS ZECHARIAH
JESUS

Christmas carol word search solution

```
Q Y M X G Y W W J W M U G J R X L P Q J W H Q
R M X H R U N X D K C W U Q S C X K K C N N Z
Z X D T Y B I R L E H W E V M P B A D B K P F
O F G H A I V H W C C F P T H K V Z P V E E M
T H G I N T N E L I S K T N H N S T C Q S Y R
B K L X J N N N J R K N T K P R G W A X D V Z
D R A G H B A S G P W D E H P N E Z C N D S T
A V I S O C F I E X Z T W V E I N E B B M G P
C P D S M G R O K S C A Z D J H J Q K D S R I
N W O T E L T T I L O O H A O L A P E I F V C
G B B G U N I O L L W Q T W L C V L G X N P J
G K W N B F U G Q L A C B P A S X X L K Q G J
A W A Y I N A M A N G E R N M A E N I S G I S
D I N G D O N G M E R R I L Y O N H I G H E X
G N I S S L E G N A D L A R E H E H T K R A H
O N C E I N R O Y A L D A V I D S C I T Y T L
K B L L K N N G S B T E W M G I S C F Q E V Z
T J H C B B I J A V S L Y R E P C Y C A D B I
A Y W X Z W H V E G Y Z A H G B M R C B V A V
H M A Z V U L V U P H S N I X K X P H S I R P
X W K K O C O M E A L L Y E F A I T H F U L X
O Q J N N T H E F I R S T N O W E L L O Y Q V
C F I R K L V U G T Z J P M D Z Z G S B F T I
```

AWAY IN A MANGER
DECK THE HALLS
DING DONG MERRILY ON HIGH
HARK THE HERALD ANGELS SING
O COME ALL YE FAITHFUL
O LITTLE TOWN
ONCE IN ROYAL DAVID'S CITY
SILENT NIGHT
THE FIRST NOWELL
WE THREE KINGS

Index of activities

About Faith in Homes

www.faithinhomes.org.uk

The Faith in Homes ministry includes three elements—resourcing, researching and signposting.

Resourcing

Living out the Christian faith at home may not seem easy for families. Our hope is that you will find the Faith in Homes website a place of easy-to-use ideas, resources, events and links to other websites to help you live out your faith together. The Barnabas Children's Ministry Team is passionate about finding a variety of ways to encourage and support all families.

This website is also for church leaders who share our vision of helping to nurture faith in the home. We offer a wide range of relevant articles, publications and research, as well as support and practical ways for churches to encourage faith within the home.

Researching

Alongside all of this, we are actively researching new ways and approaches to support faith within the home. We are asking questions such as:

What is needed to encourage and resource faith to happen or develop further in the home?

What are the challenges faced?

How can 'church' and 'home' work together to support families?

The answers to these and other questions will enable us to meet the needs of families of all styles and backgrounds.

Signposting

In addition to all the material available on the Faith in Homes website, you will also find links to resources, events, organisations and other websites that may be of interest.

About the author

Jane Butcher is responsible for developing the Faith in Homes ministry, which is something she has a passion and vision for, both as a member of the Barnabas Children's Ministry Team and as a parent. She has a desire that parents, church leaders and others share in this ministry and feel encouraged, supported and resourced to engage with such an important area.

Jane originally trained and worked as a teacher, but moved into church ministry in 1993. She has a wide range of experience in schools and churches from her posts in both the UK and USA. She has led training sessions and seminars in a variety of schools, churches and dioceses on many different aspects of RE and children's ministry, and is also an accredited Godly Play Teacher.